Ways to Find Your Way

Types of Maps

by Kay Jackson

Consultant: Susanna A. McMaster, PhD
Associate Director, MGIS Program
Geography Department, University of Minnesota

Squawk! Oh, I mean hi! I'm Ace McCaw. I love maps! Come on, I'll show you why.

Capstone
press

Mankato, Minnesota

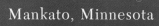

First Facts is published by Capstone Press
1710 Roe Crest Drive, North Mankato, Minnesota 56003
www.capstonepub.com

Library of Congress Cataloging-in-Publication Data
Jackson, Kay, 1959–
    Ways to find your way : types of maps / by Kay Jackson.
    p. cm.—(First facts. Map mania)
    Summary: "Describes different types of maps and how they can be used to find your
way"—Provided by publisher.
    Includes bibliographical references.
    ISBN-13: 978-1-4296-0058-3 (hardcover)
    ISBN-10: 1-4296-0058-6 (hardcover)
    ISBN-13: 978-1-4296-2882-2 (softcover pbk.)
    ISBN-10: 1-4296-2882-0 (softcover pbk.)
    1. Maps—Juvenile literature. I. Title.
GA105.6.J33 2008
912.01'4—dc22   2006100007

Editorial Credits
Jennifer Besel, editor; Linda Clavel, Veronica Bianchini, and Bobbi J. Wyss, designers;
    Bob Lentz, illustrator; Wanda Winch, photo researcher; Renée Doyle, map designer

Photo and Map Credits
Capstone Press/Karon Dubke, cover (all), 8 (globe), 15, 21
Courtesy of Play & Park Structures, 4–5 (photo)
Maps.com, 4–5 (map)
NASA/USGS/MOLA Science Team, 20
Peter Arnold, Inc./Jim Wark, 11 (photo)
Photodisc, 8–9 (background)
Topozone.com, 16 (map)
Wyoming Aero Photo/Rita Donham, 16–17 (photo)

Printed in the United States of America in Stevens Point, Wisconsin.
072013 007585R

Table of Contents

Picture This

You're a bird. (Okay, you're not. But pretend you are.) You're flying above the school. Look down at the playground. Can you see it? Well, what you see as a bird is a lot like what you see on a map. A map is a picture of the world from a bird's-eye view.

Washington Elementary School

Key
- school
- house
- playground
- tree

N W E S

| 0 | 15 | 30 | 45 | 60 feet |
| 0 | 4.5 | 9 | 13.5 | 18 meters |

Map It!

You can make a map of anything. Grab some paper and a pencil. Draw a picture of your room. Then make an X where the good hiding spots are. Now you have a map of hiding spots. Just don't leave this map out when you're playing hide-and-seek!

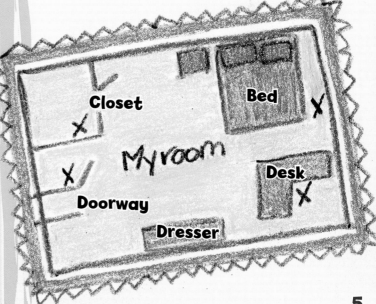

Closet

Bed

X

X

My room

Desk

X

Doorway

X

Dresser

Top Secret Map Information

Maps have all kinds of strange drawings. This **political map** has blue curvy lines all over. What do they mean? Well, I'm going to let you in on four secret details. These details will help you understand the weird drawings on any map. Ready?

political map—a map that shows where states or countries are and the dividing lines, or borders, that separate them

The **key** tells you what the symbols mean. A curvy blue line on this map stands for a river.

Key

〰 *River*

★ *Capital*

● *City*

＼ *State Border*

The United States

Montana

Missouri River

North Dakota
Bismarck ✶   Fargo

Minnesota

Billings

South Dakota
Pierre ✶
Sioux Falls ●

Wyoming

Missouri River

Casper

Minneapolis ●
St. Paul ✶

Wisconsin
Green Bay

Madison ✶

Cedar Rapids ●

Lake Superior

Lake Huron

Lake Michigan

Michigan
Lansing ✶   Detroit ●

Chicago ●

Lake Ontario

Lake Erie

Buffalo ●

New York

New York ●

husetts

viuence
Rhode Island
Hart

Connecticut

Pennsylvania

Pittsburgh ●   Harrisburg ✶

Trenton ✶

New Jersey

Dover ✶

Maps use **symbols** to stand for real things. A little black dot could be a city.

Nebraska

Omaha ●

Iowa
Des Moines ✶

Lincoln ✶

Kansas City ●   Jefferson City ✶

Illinois
Springfield ✶

Indiana
Indianapolis ✶

Fort Wayne ●

Ohio
Columbus ✶

Cincinnati ●

West Virginia
Charleston ✶

Annapolis ✶

Delaware
Maryland

Washington D.C.

City

Boulder ●
Denver ✶

Colorado

Colorado Springs ●

er

Topeka ✶

Kansas

Wichita ●

Missouri

St. Louis ●

Louisville ●   Frankfort ✶

Kentucky

Richmond ✶

Virginia

Norfolk ●

Raleigh ●

North Carolina

Charlotte ●

Cheyenne ✶

Santa Fe ✶
Albuquerque ●

New Mexico

Rio Grande

Tulsa ●
Oklahoma City ✶

Oklahoma

Fort Smith ●   Little Rock

Arkansas

Mississippi River

Nashville ✶

Tennessee

Memphis ●

Alabama

Birmingham ●

ississippi

Montgomery ✶

Atlanta ✶

Macon ●

Georgia

South Caro
Col ✶

The **compass rose** shows the directions north, south, east, and west. Keep north on top and you won't look at the map upside down.

The **scale** tells you how to figure out real distances from the tiny map. One inch on the map might equal 500 miles on the earth.

Tallahassee ✶

Florida

Miami ●

500 Kilometers

0   500 miles

Scale

N

W   E

S

7

A Round Map?

There are many types of maps. One kind is round and spins. I'm talking about a **globe**. Globes are the only maps that show the earth just as it looks from space. But globes don't show us roads or libraries. To see that information we'll need to use other types of maps.

globe—a round map that shows where the land and oceans are on the earth

Our Hero, the City Map

You need to get to the library. But then it hits you. You don't know where the library is. City map will save the day!

A city map shows where things are in a town. Symbols mark churches, stores, and lots of other spots. Check out the key on this city map. See the books? Find that symbol on the map and you'll find the library.

Island Pond, Vermont

Key

 Store

 Library

 Church

House

0   50 feet

15 meters

Walnut Avenue

North Street

Middle Street

N
W — E
S

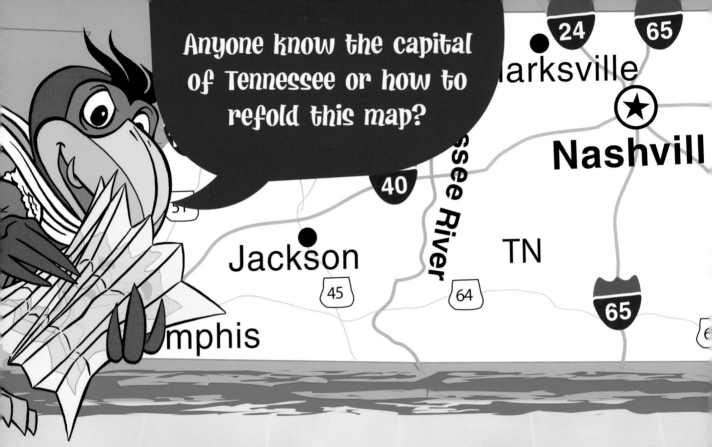

The Tour Guide: Road Maps

I love road trips! But sometimes I get lost. That's when a road map is handy. These maps show highways and other roads. They also mark state borders.

Road maps show towns, lakes, and rivers too. And symbols label all these things. A circle with a star in it points out a state's capital.

Bumpy, Lumpy Physical Maps

The earth is bumpy! Physical maps show land **features** like mountains, lakes, and rivers. Colors and symbols help us see these different parts of the land. Rivers and lakes are almost always colored blue.

Colors also show how high or low things are. Green means the land is flat. Brown marks hills and super tall mountains.

Birdsville

Migration Mountains

Feather River

Key

Mountain

Hill

Bird Feeder

Bird House

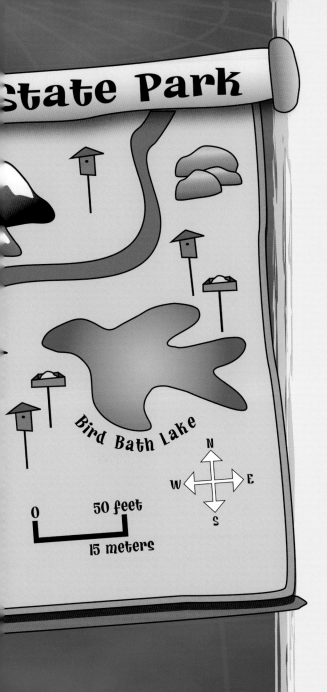

Bird Bath Lake

N
W — E
S

0   50 feet

15 meters

Map It!

Your face has high and low spots too. And you can map them. Have someone take a photo of your face. On the photo, color the high and low parts. Use the same color for spots that are the same height.

KEY

lowest spots

highest spots

15

Devils Tower National Monument

N
W · E
S

4200
4251
4200
4262
BM 4249.6
Devils Tower
5112
HIKING
Belle Fourche River

Scale

915 meters

0   3,000 feet

Key

☐ Forested Area

☐ Unforested Area

- - - - Hiking Trail

〰 Road

Pond

River

Topo-rific Maps

Topographic maps are a kind of physical map. These maps are used to see the shape of a place and how the land goes up and down. Many topo maps use **contour lines**. If the lines are far apart, you're looking at flat land. But as the lines get closer together, the more the land rises.

topographic map—a map that shows the shape of a place and the height of the land

contour lines—the brown lines on a topographic map that mark land of a certain height

17

Counting on a Map: Distribution Maps

Maps can show lots of things besides roads and bumpy land.

Distribution maps show where certain things live or grow. Need to know where the most people live? Check out a population density map. Colors on this map show how many people live in each area.

Maps are great tools to help you find what you need. So go explore the world using all kinds of maps.

distribution map—a map that shows where things, not places, are located; they can also show how much of something is in an area.

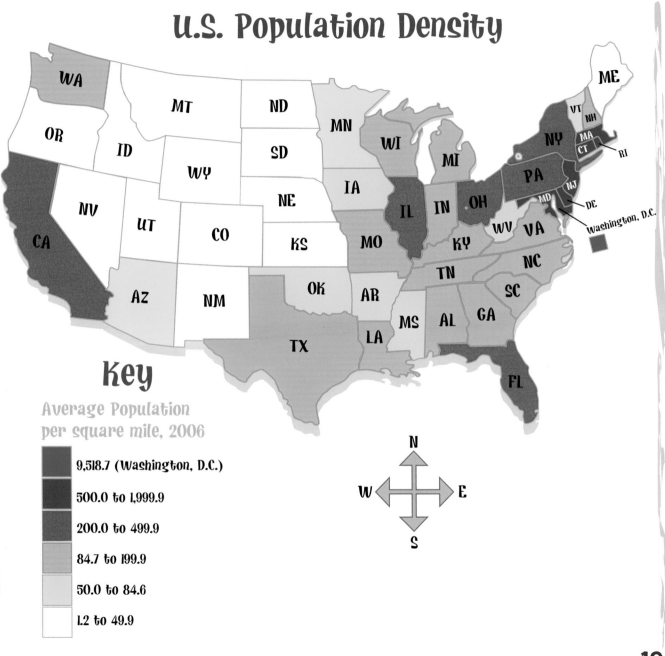

U.S. Population Density

Key

Average Population per square mile, 2006

- 9,518.7 (Washington, D.C.)
- 500.0 to 1,999.9
- 200.0 to 499.9
- 84.7 to 199.9
- 50.0 to 84.6
- 1.2 to 49.9

Scientists make maps of things in space too. In 1996, NASA sent up the *Mars Global Surveyor* spacecraft. This spacecraft had a camera on it, which took more than 240,000 pictures of the planet Mars. From the pictures, scientists were able to make a physical map of Mars.

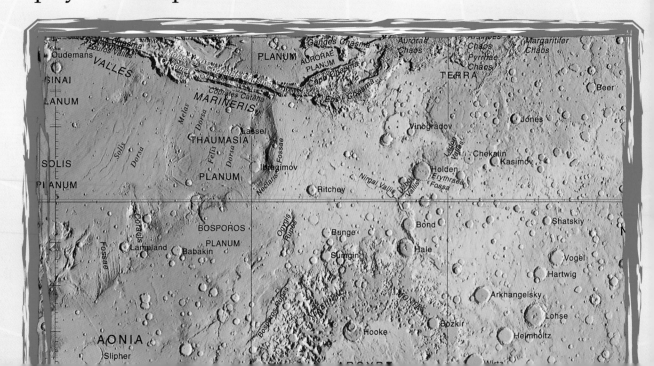

Hands On: Your Neighborhood

When you draw any kind of map, you include things that are important to you. But what's special to one person may not be to another. That means maps of the same place could be very different.

What You Need

white paper or poster board
colored pencils or markers

What You Do

1. Before you begin, ask a friend to do this activity too.
2. Draw a map of your neighborhood on the paper. Be sure to include your home, important places, and roads. Important places might be your school, a mall, or a relative's home. Don't look at your friend's map. You'll do that later.
3. Write the names of the places and roads on your map. If you use symbols, make sure to include a key.
4. When you're finished, switch maps with your friend. Compare the two maps.

Did you mark the same spots as your friend? Why are your maps different?

Glossary

contour line (KON-toor LINE)—a line on a topographic map that shows how high the land is in certain places

distribution map (diss-tri-BYOO-shun MAP)—a map that shows where groups of things live or grow

feature (FEE-chur)—an important part or quality of something

globe (GLOHB)—a round model of the world

political map (pul-LI-ti-kuhl MAP)—a map that shows the locations of countries or states and the borders between them

topographic map (top-uh-GRAF-ik MAP)—a map that shows the heights and positions of a place

Read More

Blevins, Wiley. *Maps.* Compass Point Phonics Readers. Minneapolis: Compass Point Books, 2004.

Deboo, Ana. *Mapping Your Way.* Map Readers. Chicago: Heinemann, 2007.

Mahaney, Ian F. *Map It: A Kid's Guide to Map Skills and Symbols.* Map It. New York: Rosen, 2006.

Internet Sites

FactHound offers a safe, fun way to find Internet sites related to this book. All of the sites on FactHound have been researched by our staff.

Here's how:
1. Visit *www.facthound.com*
2. Choose your grade level.
3. Type in this book ID **1429600586** for age-appropriate sites. You may also browse subjects by clicking on letters, or by clicking on pictures and words.
4. Click on the **Fetch It** button.

Facthound will fetch the best sites for you!

Index